Vancouver's Plum and Cherry Blossoms: A Spring Delight

Even our Canada geese buddies have taken a liking to sweet cherry plum blossoms. They were seen here pecking and feeding on fallen cherry blossom petals from the flowering tree at Jericho beach.

Vancouver's Plum and Cherry Blossoms: A Spring Delight

Rowena Kong

Annie Ho

Rowena Kong
2024

First Printing: 2024

ISBN: 978-1-998518-18-0

Introduction

Here is a photography journey through Vancouver's flora rich season of spring from March through April showcasing the beauty of cherry blossom("sakura" in its native Japanese language) flowers in bloom throughout this nature-loving city. A nature's paradise in the province of British Columbia, Canada, Vancouver is blessed with one of the mildest weather conditions year-round in the country. Locals and tourists alike enjoy the sight of a tremendous variety of flowers blooming from late winter through autumn in this heart-warming urban centre, also a divine gift to satisfy any garden lover. Enjoy a portion of this photography wonder through the various images captured during this spring season featuring the latest blossoms gracing Vancouver's many tree-lined streets and spacious garden parks that will delight your day.

Budding for a new season…

Plum Blossom (*Prunus Mume)* and Cherry Blossom (*Prunus serrulata)*

The months of March and April witness the streets of Vancouver basked in blooms of white, pink, ad red with the arrival of sweet plum and cherry blossom season. The Vancouver Cherry Blossom Festival is a city-wide celebration of activities that capture the joy and pleasure brought about by such tempting beauty of the flowers that have provided much cultural significance for Japan, and now well appreciated by us Vancouverites.

A bright and sunny blue sky offers the perfect backdrop to this captivating pink cherry plum blossom which blooms in mid-March. Yet, with unusually optimal weather conditions, the blooms could appear as early as late February.

A symbol of strength and resilience following the bitter chills of winter, these early plum blossoms lead the series of vibrant blooms well into late spring.

The tall and wide spreading of stunning pinks like angels' wings grace the enlivening early spring sky, coloring the land with promising hope of new vitality.

With soft tender petals as pure and white as snow, this Prunus species exudes beauty in its magnificent form, inspiring tales and legends as ancient and foretelling as the history of time.

Peak season bloom of these endearing cherry plum blossoms coincides with invigorating bright blues backdrop to present perfect nature visuals for the world…

Bursting forth with strong crisp scent, this late-bloomer plum species offers a stunning display of long stamens and rich white petals.

With outstretched branches reaching high and upwards to the skies, plum blossoms ambitiously contrast with weeping cherry blossoms in a classic way…

Early stages of bloom for this soft pink Prunus Okame cherry during the first weeks of March may be just as attractive and splendid as its later peak bloom.

A contrast of pink and white early bloomers on a bright and radiant March midday.

An early bloomer, this Prunus Okame cherry blossom is close to its peak bloom as early as the first week of March, marking the unofficial start of the spring season in mild Vancouver.

"Akebono" flower buds are a conspicuous pink, though they usually bloom to full bright white. Under the mercy of the weather, showers and rain caused the above newly bloomed petals to droop under the heavy weight of water.

These towering "Akebono" cherry trees produce mainly white blossoms and are popularly located in many residential areas. However, unwise early trimming of many of its branches has likely compromised its usual glorious spread of canopy.

A daylight half-moon in the distant lends additional element to the backdrop of this Akebono in the latter half of its peak bloom.

The chickadee bird loves the cherry blossoms, and often spends time on its trees amongst the flowers, delighting itself with them throughout the course of the season…

An early morning refresh for this fluffy sweetie as it perches on the firm branch of this late mid-April Sakura…

The "Accolade" cherry (Prunus "Accolade") begins blooming a little earlier and at just about the same time as the Akebono in the late weeks of March, with more eye-catching soft pink hue and yellow hearts that exude charming feminine beauty. Their towering trees stand strong and tall reaching the height of streetlights, creating an impressive sight for scenery lovers.

A wonder that merges beauty and strength, the "Accolade" cherry earns itself great popularity and fame amongst the cultivars.

Well into and beyond their peak bloom, these Akebono Yoshino cherry blossoms have their snowy white petals transforming into soft pink hues, further enhancing their feminine representation of beauty in mid-spring April.

With green leaves gradually replacing the blooms, these Akebono trees by a residential area sidewalk seize their chance to flourish in exuberant pinks for another feast of delight before an impending conclusion for the year.

Queen Elizabeth Park Garden

The Akebono Yoshino cherry trees at Queen Elizabeth Park Garden welcome their first blooms from late March to early April and maintain its lasting favourite spot for hanami amongst the locals and out-of-town visitors.

Spreading tall and wide, the sturdy blossom trees of the park provide a sheltering canopy of awe and beauty and a means for stress relief in the midst of an overwhelming pandemic period.

Also a five-petaled beauty, this greenish white blossom reaches peak bloom shortly after the Akebonos in late April.

"Yaezakura," which denotes cherry blossoms with more than five petals for each flower, bloom after the Somei Yoshino in the later half of the month of April into May. The more common kinds usually have a deeper pink colour of petals, which contrasts with the lighter whites of Yoshino cherry.

Breathtaking shades of pink and white of this late bloomer paint a marvel of oriental nature as these blooms grace an inconspicuous street corner against the backdrop of an overcast sky.

With deep red centres adding contrast to the many yellowish white petals, each heavy
bundle of blossoms gives a fuller view of the tree's peak bloom.

A close up view of drooping Shiro-fugen with its copper brown leaves against the backdrop of bright pink Kanzan Yaezakura blooms.

The abundant bright pink blooms of the Kanzan arrive during the second last week of April, lining streets with generous amount of colour a hallmark of vibrant spring.

Fallen petals of sweet bridal pink Kanzan Yaezakura spread over and carpeted a bright green grassy ground as the bloom nears its end in the last week of April, a splendid fairy tale-like scene in a commonplace Vancouver housing neighbourhood.

A stunning Kikuzakura, the Japanese term for cherry blossoms with more numerous petals than the Yaezakura, pictured here at one of Vancouver's endearing beaches, the Jericho beach in the West Point Grey neighbourhood, exudes its full bright pinkish white bloom in early May. It appears that the number of flower petals in bloom from various species increases with time of the season, beginning with five-petaled Akebonos in mid-March to the most numbered of Kikuzakuras in May.